T0150749

Finding Forever *love*

Praise for

Finding Forever *love*

"Jodi does it again. Her organized approach to tackling a difficult subject keeps the reader turning the pages of her new book. She doesn't shy away from sharing her own story, with its pitfalls, learnings and ultimate reward—a great relationship with the love of her life."

–Judith P.

"The sharing of Jodi's own story in *Finding Forever Love* was powerfully insightful and will be a guiding light for those in search of true meaningful love. I found the book to be light-hearted and full of perception, as it is jammed packed with wisdom, common sense, practical examples, and a few surprises. I felt warm in knowing Jodi cares for a woman's well-being. She's right there with you and has your back every step of the way!"

–Beth Ann Thada

"*Finding Forever Love* is a no-nonsense self-help book full of engaging stories, tools, and tips on overcoming any obstacles you might be facing in the world of dating. The 7-step FOREVER Framework is your guide, and the steps are clear and concise. It is an introspective journey to take to challenge yourself to look at your belief systems on dating, while acknowledging the knowledge and strengths you already possess. The best part of the book is that it addresses any fears or self-doubt you may have, and provides you with strategies to successfully find your forever love. It's a must-read for any gal searching for Mr. Right."

–Joanne Noruzi

"*Finding Forever Love* is refreshingly honest, sent from the soul, and is no-holds-barred to the point. I appreciated all the personal stories used as examples, because it told me I'm not the only one experiencing those types of dates. Thanks for this very valuable information!"

–Sharon Sohr

"Where was this book years ago? *Finding Forever Love* is clear and concise regarding what to do to find Mr. Right. The author's advice is very practical and helpful. So often, we try to change the man, or change who we are, to make it work. We forget who we are, all for a man. It's a slippery slope. Dating takes thought, intention, and a big load of grace! This is a book to help us be clear with our intentions in all our relationships."

–Ellen Krumenauer

"Answers are hard to find when you are questioning yourself and looking for reasons to doubt yourself. Using her FOREVER Framework, Jodi shows the reader that doubting yourself is normal after relationship breakdown. The FOREVER Framework allows you to embrace the doubt and turn it into finding Mr. Right. Written from the heart, this book guides the reader to turn hurt into a path forward to where you will find Mr. Right."

Finding Forever

*7 Steps to Your
Mr. Right*

Jodi Schuelke

NEW YORK

LONDON • NASHVILLE • MELBOURNE • VANCOUVER

Finding Forever *love*
7 Steps to Your Mr. Right

Published in New York, New York, by Morgan James Publishing in partnership with Difference Press. Morgan James is a trademark of Morgan James, LLC. www.MorganJamesPublishing.com

ISBN 978-1-64279-346-8 paperback
ISBN 978-1-64279-347-5 eBook
Library of Congress Control Number: 2018913195

Cover Design by:
Rachel Lopez
www.r2cdesign.com

Interior Design by:
Bonnie Bushman
The Whole Caboodle Graphic Design

In an effort to support local communities, raise awareness and funds, Morgan James Publishing donates a percentage of all book sales for the life of each book to Habitat for Humanity Peninsula and Greater Williamsburg.

Get involved today! Visit
www.MorganJamesBuilds.com

Dedication

To the many very special people in my life who have shown me the meaning of grace.

To the few very difficult people who have taught me how to "love in spite of."

And especially, to my beloved husband, Dan, whose balance and unconditional love help me appreciate the miracles in every relationship–the loving and supportive, and the challenging.

Table of Contents

	Introduction	*xi*
Chapter 1	My Story	1
Chapter 2	Step 1: Futurize Your Success	11
Chapter 3	Step 2: Own Your Power	21
Chapter 4	Step 3: Review and Reset	30
Chapter 5	Step 4: Evaluate Your Date	47
Chapter 6	Step 5: Value Your Vision	61
Chapter 7	Step 6: Establish Your Independence	72
Chapter 8	Step 7: Respect Reality	79
Chapter 9	Your Transformation	88
Chapter 10	Conclusion	92
	Acknowledgments	*97*
	About the Author	*100*
	Thank You!	*102*

Introduction

If you've picked up this book, it's my hunch you're wanting to re-enter the dating scene so you can find *your* Mr. Right and ultimately get married again. You've longed to find the exact man with whom you can share your life—someone who is your best friend, a satisfying lover, your emotional support, and a man that you can trust and depend on—a true life partner.

But somewhere in the back of your mind, there's still a flicker of doubt. You want to return to dating, but you're afraid. You don't want to waste your time on guys who aren't a good fit. You're afraid to take that step forward and put yourself out there for fear you won't know what to do or where to look. You might get let down or hurt again. Even worse, maybe nobody will be interested in you.

Finding Forever Love is about focusing your attention and dating with intention, so you can find your future life partner.

You'll know what to look for and why, where to look, and how to put yourself out there so that you don't attract the wrong types of guys again and waste precious time. It's the sure-fire way to create changes and shifts in your dating strategy that will lay a new foundation for finding your Mr. Right—and achieve lasting results.

When you know how to create those changes and strategy shifts, the only remaining questions are: *How good of a relationship can you stand?* and *How long do you want to wait to start toward having it?*

What It Really Takes

There's a lot that goes into setting a new goal, stepping away from bad habits, and staying focused. It starts with having a strategy, which includes the process structure and the tactics, but it also includes self-love, trust, and being attuned to your intuition. You'll have to learn to walk both paths—understanding the concepts and the parameters, but also being aware of ways you might self-sabotage.

This book takes you through strategies to help you step back into the dating arena with confidence. We wrap up with a look at what your life can be like on the other side—when you've found your Mr. Right. All of it is designed to help you implement the concepts in such a way that they become second nature.

You're not going to find your own sense of balance, however, until you actually go through the FOREVER Framework™ process. There will most likely be challenges, but I'm certain there will be many more victories.

You may be tempted to read this and try to cherry-pick and implement only *some* of the steps, but I guarantee it won't work. The only way you'll be able to learn and change your relationship future is to fully step into the FOREVER Framework process and make it happen. It may be scary, but it's absolutely worth it—and that's going to be the value of completing it. This, my friend, is going to transform your love life!

Meet Lisa

Lisa is an educated and goal-driven career woman who left corporate America a few years ago to teach business classes at a local university. She's the busy single mom of two teenage boys who are both very active in school sports. Lisa was married once before to her college sweetheart, the father of her children.

Shortly after finishing college, Lisa got pregnant and had her first son. She had her second two years later. She soon realized that her husband preferred to be anywhere else but home, helping raise their kids. And when he was home, things were tense and stressful. Following a few years of trying to get him to be more present as a husband and father, Lisa finally ended the marriage upon learning that her husband had been cheating on her. Fortunately, their divorce was amicable, and they've been able to co-parent with limited drama.

At the time I met Lisa, she had been divorced for almost seven years. During that time, she'd dated casually and had a few short-term and a couple of longer-term relationships. Even though she'd been on a variety of dating sites, she seemed to attract similar types of guys—narcissists, commitment-phobes, playboys, and those with compulsive or addictive personalities and the problems that went with them: alcohol, gambling, work problems, and more. Lisa's boys struggled with some of her boyfriends, and then behaved disrespectfully toward her. After a string of *not-the-right-fit* relationships, increased tension with her boys, and feeling like her dating and home life were a total train wreck, Lisa came to the realization that *she* had to make some serious changes, and fast.

Lisa discovered my second book, *Relationship Detox: 7 Steps to Prepare for Your Ideal Relationship*, and found it was exactly what she needed to help her stop the crazy dating cycle she'd been in for so long. She was excited, but nervous, about doing the detox on her own, and she knew that she wanted an accountability partner to help her through the process to ensure that she'd be successful and not slide backward. Lisa wanted to get it right the first time, not only for herself, but also for her boys' sakes.

During the time we worked together, Lisa was able to really examine her past relationships and clearly see the unhealthy patterns. She was able to formulate her vision for what she *did* ideally want in a future relationship partner. She was also able to be more present for her boys and to feel more emotionally connected to them again.

After a few months, Lisa was ready to try dating again, but she was worried that she might not be able to discern the good guys from the bad, would slip back into old patterns and habits, and would end up dating the same old wastes of time again.

With ongoing support and guidance, Lisa developed a brand-new dating strategy that enabled her to meet her *Mr. Right* in no time at all.

The Risks

For Lisa, the obvious risks were falling back into those old dating patterns, dating unfit men, wasting her time, and jeopardizing finding her happily ever after. In addition, her *pre-relationship detox* lifestyle had significantly affected her relationship with her boys. Lisa knew she wanted to be married again, but this time to the right man—someone she could feel proud of, someone her kids would welcome and accept, and someone who would be a positive male role model. She knew getting serious about dating meant she'd have to be vigilant about reaching her goal, and that it would include the risks of it taking a while, of possibly getting rejected, and of being tempted to settle for an *average* guy versus being patient and waiting for her Mr. Right.

You, too, may be feeling nervous about the unknown. You may have doubts that you will ever meet a decent guy—like maybe you don't really deserve it. You may worry that you're not young enough, pretty enough, smart enough, skinny enough, or sexy enough to meet a great man. Or, you're unsure any even exist. You may not believe you can do this and follow through on making these changes because any previous quick-fix attempts to break these patterns left you feeling lonely and depressed, which resulted in you sliding backward and settling for unavailable or unfit men, again. You may even have a sick feeling in your stomach from worrying about how to implement *new* dating strategies, let alone how to know where to even start.

Sweetheart, I totally get it. I know how hard it is to change course, take risks, go in search of a big dream, and create a new life. I understand where you've been, because I've been there, too.

There's nothing wrong with wanting to find *the man of your dreams* and to live your happily ever after together, but moving toward that vision can be scary.

Fear is a natural instinct and is intended to keep us safe, but when you hide behind fear versus utilizing it as a catalyst for change, you'll stay stuck in the same old, dead-end patterns and continue to feel miserable.

I know you have all you need within you, my dear, and you *can* do this.

The Reward

Choosing to stop the insanity, step away from past unhealthy habits, and set course in a different direction will be the beginning of a beautiful transformation for you—a gift to yourself.

Imagine a life where you are in an emotionally healthy and loving relationship with a man you trust and adore. Where you feel calm, content and secure, and are free to fully be yourself. Where you are accepted and cherished and loved unconditionally. A relationship where you spend your free time creating a life and making fun memories together with your partner. You are able to pursue any of your goals and dreams, and you have someone in your life who wants the best for you and is always cheering you on.

Gone will be the days of endless searching, convincing, chasing, or shape shifting yourself to fit another man's preference or fantasy, because you won't need to do that anymore—it won't even matter—and you'll be able to breathe easy.

Life will be so much better when your only regret is that you didn't make this change years ago.

I Will Show You the Way

This book chronicles the strategic dating journey I went on after my relationship detox, and how I finally found the relationship of my dreams and got married again. Any mistakes and missteps I experienced along the way are also shared, which I hope will help you to better navigate the process, so you can powerfully transform your life.

I've also included case studies about clients I've coached, as well as insights from mental health professionals and knowledge I gained from two decades of research on dating and relationships. My wish is that this book will help you cross over to a better and healthier love life and a more promising future.

What's to Come

In *Finding Forever Love*, we're going to explore the seven steps of the FOREVER Framework process. These have been strategically designed to help you take your dating strategy and love life to the next level. Over the course of this book, I will walk you through the exact steps I took when I got serious about dating and finding my Mr. Right, who became my husband. I'll share the concepts and strategies that took me years to develop and learn, including mistakes I made and tactics I used to keep me on track.

There are seven steps, each of which is designed to walk you through a mapped-out plan and set you up to find your future husband.

As you read through this book, I invite you to trust the process.

Chapter 1

My Story

*I*n my second book, *Relationship Detox*, I shared the story of my post-divorce, post-rebound relationship healing phase—the story of when I finally got sick and tired of wasting my time with unfit men and how I was able to detox from my unhealthy dating patterns and habits. *Finding Forever Love* is the culmination of my dating experiences (and those of my clients). It tells how I found my Mr. Right and got married again.

My 30s Gone Wild

After the dust settled from that rebound relationship break-up, I decided to try online dating to see what that was like. I signed up for Match.com, created my profile, and started meeting some men and having conversations. I wasn't really sure what I was looking for, but I just knew the next guy couldn't be *anything* like my last two exes.

Soon I was chatting online, then talking on the phone with a few different guys, and finally I started going out on dates. I wasn't particularly picky—if they were remotely attractive and didn't come across as some total pervert or creepy type, I was open to having a conversation. I found myself enjoying the attention, flirting, meeting new men online and in person, and getting more dating experience. You could say I had more of a, *"Hi, You'll Do"* attitude, at first.

Most of the guys were very nice initially, and I enjoyed the conversation and their company, but I found that some were more interested in me than I was in them. I met a few jerks along the way, and even unknowingly dated a married guy who ghosted on me after a month.

I did have a few back-to-back serious relationships with different guys for spans ranging from a few months to half a year. I worked hard to keep them moving forward by suggesting or making plans for us to do fun activities together. I would also help them out whenever I could, prioritizing their needs over mine, and even over my kids' needs. But when the relationship started to fall apart, I'd do everything I could to try to fix things, even if that meant me trying to change who *I* was. But that act never lasted long. I ended up feeling resentful that they were losing interest, and frustrated that I wasted time *again* with someone who wasn't the right fit.

As I gained more experience meeting and dating various types of guys, I became more selective.

The Last Straw

My *30s Gone Wild* phase went on for about six years. To outsiders, it looked like a revolving door of dates and relationships. I was growing exhausted from searching so hard and continuously settling for *not-the-right-fit* guys. What I didn't quite realize at the time was that I was learning a ton about men, dating, relationships, and also about myself. I was figuring out what I ultimately wanted and transforming into the person I was destined to become.

The end of *that* lifestyle happened when I began seeing a guy I'll call Dean. We got matched up on e-Harmony, and, true to form, I took the initiative and reached out to him first. We chatted online for a week or so, then talked on the phone, and from there he asked me out on an early dinner date. He seemed decent and respectable, so we met.

It was springtime, so we decided to meet at a riverside café and sit outside to enjoy the warmer weather and catch the sunset. Since it was the start of the baseball season and he'd said he was a huge fan, I was cool with him periodically checking his phone for score updates throughout our conversation. We ordered dinner and some drinks, and were enjoying a nice conversation and getting more acquainted with one another. It was Happy Hour with a two-for-one drink special and, before I knew it, I was feeling tipsy.

Dean seemed very nice, and I found him relatively attractive. When it was time to leave the café, I invited him back to my house to watch a movie and continue our conversation. Well, thanks to the alcohol, feeling lonely, and not having had sex in quite a while, I went against my better judgment and slept with him that night.

Fast forward to our third date—Dean invited me to go for a day-long boat ride. I was looking forward to it, but much to my surprise he showed up to my house with a fishing boat. I hadn't been fishing since I was a kid, but thought, *Sure. Why not?* I suspected he was using it as an opportunity to test me, which was later confirmed when he said, "You're only the third girl I've ever taken out fishing, so that says a lot about what I think of you." I found that both interesting and a bit odd, but I made the most of the experience.

Dean was surprised to find that I was enjoying myself and wasn't afraid to put a worm on the hook. After a while I was pulling in fish that seemed bigger than the couple he'd caught. He took a break from fishing, and I noticed him checking his phone. Within a few moments it was apparent he was not checking baseball scores. Dean was deep into texting mode with someone and was sporting an expression that tipped me off it was most likely another female. So, I casually asked who he was having so much fun chatting with. He stumbled over his words like he'd just gotten busted, and said it was his son. Dean's demeanor quickly changed, and he announced we had to wrap it up because he had to get back for his son's baseball practice.

I found this confusing, because the day before Dean had told me he never went to his 17-year-old son's practices—his son had a vehicle and drove himself. I knew better than to raise the question and just let him drop me back off at home and be on his way.

While that experience was disappointing, I wasn't feeling heartbroken or really that angry at Dean. But rather, I finally felt awakened to the reality that I was *done* with putting up with all the dating games, drama, open relationships, and basically not respecting myself. I finally set some standards for myself and started using them from the start.

How I Figured It Out

Over the next few days I thought a lot about what had happened with Dean and spent considerable time reflecting on my dating past. I wasn't angry with him, but rather I was crystal clear for the first time about what I wanted for myself and my future.

Later the next week Dean called to check in with me and see what I'd been up to because he hadn't heard from me. I took that opportunity to ask him a few questions. The first was to clarify what really happened on the boat and his urgency to get back. As it turned out, my suspicions were correct and he was actually texting with another woman he'd also been seeing at the same time. She'd ended up getting the night off of work and was able to go out on a date with him after all. Dean prided himself in being honest with me after the fact.

The next question I asked was, "What are your intentions?"— which he didn't seem to understand—so I re-phrased it to, "So what is it you really want from me?" His reply was, "I don't know what I want. I'm still trying to figure that out. But I like you."

In the past I would've thought, *"Awesome, he likes me!"* and I would've worked my butt off to try to prove to the guy that I was a keeper. But not anymore. Instead I said, "Yeah. Makes sense. Well, I happen to know what it is I want, which is a serious committed relationship with a man who's actually interested in having the same thing with me. And I want to get married again."

Dean got defensive and said that he wasn't ready for all that yet and asked if I could give him time so he could figure out what he wanted.

I told him no and said that I wasn't going to wait around for him—or any guy for that matter—to figure things out, that I knew what I wanted and I was going to move on so I could find it. I politely thanked him for the few nice dates, wished him the best of luck in figuring things out, and said good-bye.

That experience honestly helped wake me up to what I really wanted for myself and the type of *man* I wanted in my life.

The FOREVER Framework

What I learned, by leaving my *30s Gone Wild* dating phase behind and taking the steps to break free of those poor dating patterns and do a complete 180 degree turn, isn't for the weak-hearted, but it was absolutely worth it. I had to first admit I was the one responsible for my dating faux pas and unhappiness. I had to set a new goal. And then I had to become a woman who felt and behaved like she already had the man of her dreams, in order to be able to attract him. That meant I had to get crystal clear on what I ultimately wanted, step into my power, fully embrace the new changes, and work hard to keep myself focused and on track.

I had a responsibility to myself, as an intelligent woman and as a mother, to model healthy choices and actions for my kids. I was willing to take the necessary steps and potential risks to give us a better future. And that's exactly what I want for you—a better and love-filled future.

I've pooled all my experience and trial-and-error efforts, research, and my clients' experiences, as well as insights from relationship experts, into the seven steps of the FOREVER Framework process. It's what I wish I had years ago to guide me through transforming my dating life faster, so it would've been easier and wouldn't have taken so long to find my wonderful second husband.

The following chapters walk you through each of the steps of the FOREVER Framework, including to-dos, how-tos, what to avoid, and why the steps are important. Based on your personal situation, you can select the things that resonate most for you.

The FOREVER Framework is an easy-to-follow guide intended to help you successfully revamp your dating strategy. It can help you better prepare, based on your personal situation. It can also help you keep your wits about you while you're going through this transformational process.

I will be right here, in this book, walking alongside you throughout your journey. You can trust that this process will help you reach your goal of finding high quality dating prospects so that you can finally find *your* Mr. Right. It can also help you open up space, so you can create the love life you've always dreamed about.

FOREVER Framework™ Steps

F = Futurize Your Success—When you know what you're aiming for, it's easier to hit the mark.

O = Own Your Power—Access the strength and knowledge you already possess.

R = Review and Reset—Become self-aware so that it's easier to make adjustments.

E = Evaluate Your Date—Know what to ask, so you can make better choices.

V = Value Your Vision—Learn how to address the challenges that can arise.

E = Establish Your Independence—Grow into your new, healthier patterns.

R = Respect Reality—Navigate life once you've met your Mr. Right.

What to Expect Along Your Journey

As you read through the following chapters, you may have bouts of fear or self-doubt. You will be learning new concepts and methods and things you may have never considered. Some of the information in the upcoming chapters may challenge you in ways that will scare you, maybe even make you angry. You may even want to give up, because it's hard work. Please be kind to yourself and remember that changing your dating strategy, embarking on a new beginning, and rewriting your relationship future can feel nerve-wracking. This is completely normal.

I invite you to take some time right now to evaluate where you are presently and whether you're truly ready to step forward into dating. Then go ahead, and read the remainder of this book. When you're done, check in with yourself to see how you feel. Whenever you're ready to get started, this book can help you create a new and better love life, one that works for you.

Chapter 2
Step 1: Futurize Your Success

*H*aving a healthy, loving, and fulfilling relationship with a partner is wonderful and is what I believe everyone truly wants. In order to be able to find the *right* relationship partner, you must first know what your end-goal is. You need a vision of romantic success that goes beyond the present moment or even the present year. You need to plan and act now, even before the first date, to ensure your success, not just for the short-term, but for the long run: You want to futurize your success.

In this first step, we set the stage for the remaining steps by embracing the idea that you can find your forever love. You'll succeed because you pointed yourself in the direction you really do want to go.

The end goal is to find the man who is the *right* fit for you. Many women long for a man who fits some fantasy ideal—professional athlete, celebrity, airbrushed hottie, or some Dr. McDreamy or McSteamy type. Sure, they're easy on the eyes, but the goal, or so I hope is the case for you, isn't to chase superficial qualities, but rather to find the *right* man. An emotionally mature man who is ready, able, and willing to fully commit and who wants to build a future with you. This is also a stepping stone to other opportunities in your life, too.

Putting Your Own House in Order First

Before you can begin your search for your future relationship partner, you must first have *your* house in order. Even before you can have a successful relationship with a partner, it starts with you having a healthy relationship with *yourself*. This includes focusing your attention on expanding and filling yourself with the right stuff—the right mindset, concepts, activities, and people.

Do not drop what you've already learned and jump back blindly, losing focus, and giving away all of your time and energy to just any guy. You can retain your ideal relationship—the one with yourself—while you're looking for your Mr. Forever.

All the strategy in the world won't help until you've also dealt with your personal energy and your mindset. It's about staying true to yourself and keeping your balance as you step forward into this new process.

Shift Your Attention

It's important that you take the time to connect with what you truly want in a future relationship partner, so that you don't end up back at square one again and waste considerable time and energy dating the wrong guys. Now's the time to get super honest with yourself about what it is you truly want in a relationship.

In order to futurize your success, make space in your life by taking a time-out from dating for a while. This break enables you to shift your attention *away* from those dating habits or behavioral patterns that have you feeling frustrated or stuck on the proverbial hamster wheel of missteps, failed relationships, and heartache.

During this break, shift your attention to clarifying your desired outcome. This is a time to dream and ask yourself what you really want and what you've always wished for in an ideal relationship partner. The key is to get clear in your mind and to feel it in your heart: to be able to get your desired outcome, know who you are, who you want to be, how you want to feel, and what the best-case scenario looks like.

You can do this by writing down your responses to these prompts:

- Describe your ideal relationship partner. (Include as much detail as possible. What does he look like? What does he do for a living? What is his level of education? What are his interests and hobbies? What are his goals in life? Etc.)
- Write down up to 5 reasons why you want this. (There is no right or wrong answer—these can be practical or superficial or ego reasons.)
- What are 3-5 changes you might have to make if your dream comes true? And, are you willing to make these changes?

The value of writing down your dream come true is for you to connect that with your intentions—to stay inspired and excited about the results you want to achieve. The truth of what's possible starts to arise, and this is your chance to truly change your life.

Have a Game Plan

When you're in a relationship with a guy who's emotionally unavailable, it's easy for you to display *needy* behaviors. He's not giving you what you really want, which is partnership, openness, and vulnerability. As women, when we don't get what we want from a guy, we tend to try harder by attempting to bring him closer, by making him the center of our world, or by actually trying to teach him how to be in a relationship.

As you embark on your journey to attract your future relationship partner, your chances of success are much greater if you lay out a game plan. Having a plan creates structure and helps to prevent situations where you're engaging in conversations or going on dates with guys who are not aligned with what you want. A plan helps you avoid sliding backward into old, unhealthy habits—because you'll already have that figured out.

So, the concern of having a misstep and reverting back to bad dating habits is eradicated by having a game plan, because you've decided in advance what you'll be doing. It prevents you from making excuses where you skip putting your needs first. Creating that structure will keep you from falling prey to shameful thoughts or emotion-based fears, because your strategy is already planned out.

If you stumble along the way, the challenge will be deciding if you're going to regain your footing, forgive yourself, and refocus on your game plan. Or, are you going to do what too many women do and give up and say it's too hard? The reason I'm here writing to you today is because I didn't totally give up on myself, even when it got hard and I got scared.

So regardless of whether or not you have a misstep, it'll be a great learning experience stepping back into the dating arena again.

Getting Ghosted

Lynn and Mike had been dating for a few months. She'd met him on a free dating site, right after her last break-up. They had fun together and there wasn't any drama, which felt refreshing for Lynn. After a few weeks of dating, Mike became more and more preoccupied with his job and various DIY house projects. Trying to be helpful, Lynn took more of the initiative in going to his house to visit and hang out together, and would even bring dinner over when he had to work late.

As Lynn was leaving one morning following a sleepover, Mike announced that he was going on vacation the next week to visit family back home in Michigan. He didn't invite Lynn to join him, even though he knew she was between work contracts and had the month off. She felt disappointed but was too afraid to ask him if she could come along for fear he'd say no or get mad at her. So, she instead pretended it was no big deal.

Everything else seemed fine with Mike before he left, but he didn't contact Lynn after he returned from his trip. A few days passed, and Lynn was getting concerned but wanted to play cool about it. She tried to convince herself that maybe he stayed a few days longer, but she knew better. Lynn tried calling a few different times over the next week, but Mike never answered or returned her text messages. After two weeks of unreturned callbacks, Lynn accepted the fact that she'd been ghosted.

If this has ever happened to you, I'm sure you already know that it's not fun. Ghosting can send people reeling mentally and cause them to repeatedly text or call. The more messages that are sent or left, the more dramatic, needy, or angry the one getting ghosted can feel. There are even cases where you might feel inclined to stalk the other person, whether on social media, by doing drive-bys of their home or work, or by contacting their friends to find out what's going on or seek some closure. In Lynn's situation, she never got the closure she hoped for from Mike.

Ready, Set, Repeat Mistakes

I've seen it countless times—women who take a little time out from dating and then jump right back into the game, repeating the same stuff they did before. Like Lynn, they're in such a rush about finding *a* man, and get consumed by the man they did land that they neglect to focus on whether he's *the right* man— *one* who will be the *right* fit for the long haul and whom they can spend the rest of their lives with.

Or, they find themselves on a date with some Mr. Six Pack Abs whose personality is shallower than a kiddie pool, and everything they said they wanted previously gets tossed out the window. Then later, they're frustrated when they find themselves right back where they were before. Feeling miserable and many times bitter about men.

The FOREVER Framework is not a miracle cure or quick fix formula. It's a process.

Be Honest with Yourself

Before you can take action, be realistic about what you can incorporate into your schedule and life, with an eye toward maintaining structure and balance. How much time do you have available to date? Or, how much time do you actually want to devote to finding your Mr. Right?

As you read on, keep in mind that as you prepare to step back into dating again, at any time you can pivot and go in a different direction, or take a time-out if you find yourself losing focus.

A New Plan of Action

Once you're certain about what you're aiming for, you are ready to start dating again. Now it's time to formulate a strategy, so you can have a solid game plan to follow. When you set it up in advance, you're basically declaring: this is my life and my priority, and this is how I am going to do it.

When you think of strategizing in terms of a sports team, there are issues to consider like researching the other team, strategizing, and practice that takes place before the game even starts. After the game, they look back on what happened, address the issues, and adjust their strategy to try to avoid pitfalls in the future.

The same holds true when you're getting ready to step back into the dating arena again. Having a game plan means you're less likely to get thrown by the part of you that's scared of being rejected or meeting more guys that don't fit your dream. Make sure that plan includes managing your time when you return to dating. In the process, you'll build confidence just by the fact that you were courageous enough to follow through and stick to the plan… because it's that valuable to you.

The plan is the overall strategy you'll follow that will bring about your chosen result, which in this case is finding your Mr. Right—your future husband.

Knowing in advance what outcome you want for yourself enables you to have the courage to cut your losses early without regressing backward into chasing a man or trying to convince him that you're worthy. And it enables you to be able to pivot quickly and better assess where to go from here.

~~~~~~

Futurizing your success in this way will help you to lay the necessary foundation and prepare you to find your forever love. The next chapter will help you move forward in establishing the outcome you want to achieve.

Chapter 3

Step 2: Own Your Power

Learning how to own your power is a very important, yet easy skillset that will help you in finding your Mr. Right. Taking a break from dating and getting focused on what you want for your future was an honorable decision, and I have a hunch you have more clarity now. But you may also feel a bit hesitant about learning new dating strategies, because you know they will thrust you forward into new experiences and brand-new territory.

This chapter helps you better understand how to stand in your power, be confident in what you already know, and trust yourself. When you're in your power, you know who you are, your values, and what you want your life and your future relationship to look like.

Taking this step gives you the opportunity to feel grounded in your decisions and trust your intuition.

Getting Clear

Our happiness is seeded in our various relationships—with loved ones, friends, and beyond. These close relationships tend to be easy and fun. But when you're dating and trying to find your Mr. Right, that happiness can feel far off. Or, worse, like you may never obtain it.

You can get the relationship you desire, but only if you trust *yourself*. If dating has felt like a struggle or like you've hit speed bumps or dead ends, then something's wrong. What you've been doing isn't working.

As you read on you'll learn the strategies that *feel good and easy, and are no work at all,* and that will lead you to more successful dating prospects. Finding your Mr. Right is about taking off the rose-colored glasses and getting serious about attaining your dream. This type of relationship begins with getting clear on what you truly want and what feels best to you—which you'll learn more about in the upcoming chapters.

Being Congruent

Not *all* of your success is about being on the right dating site. In fact, in my personal experience and through coaching my clients, I know that success in finding the right man is *more* about being congruent. When you're congruent, you are aligned. This means your insides and your outsides match. You live and breathe a message that you also think and believe. Your success is created from this place. And your results are in alignment with your clarity. When you're congruent, you walk your talk, you're clear, and you align your *now* with your future.

Being congruent is about being honest with yourself and is an integral piece to owning your power, and that's the true reward.

You get out of alignment when you say you want one thing, but you do something else. Misalignment also happens when you look to inexperienced people for new advice to figure out your next steps. But what happens then is you risk wasting time by chasing after mock solutions—or the wrong guys—and ultimately end up frustrated.

This happens by: trying to people please others, like dating a rich guy to impress your family or friends. And even when you try to use someone else's words in your dating profile (you slap theirs on yours in hopes that'll be a quick solution) without any in depth reflection on what you truly want. What's usually at the core is shame. Many people don't believe in themselves or think they're actually worth having an amazing relationship. They're embarrassed by their big dream, or they're embarrassed to admit they want more or someone better. So, they stuff it down to avoid the fear of making another mistake and being criticized, the pain of rejection, or even succeeding.

Maintaining Boundaries

Embarking on your journey to find your Mr. Right can feel very exciting. You can have your game plan in motion with everything going great. But even as you step into your new dating strategy and enjoy meeting new men and going on fun dates, there may be outsiders who may not fully understand what you are doing and why, and therefore judge you or offer up unsolicited advice.

One of the key things to consider when you're going through this step of the FOREVER Framework process is to not be afraid to stand up for yourself and the goal you have set, even if someone tries to say it's pointless or that you're doing it all wrong.

This is a very common issue that comes up, especially if you have friends or family who tend to want to be over-involved in your life, those who are fearful of you being single forever, or even those who have big hearts and cannot resist the urge to help those they love *be* happy. They mean well, but if you don't establish boundaries with these individuals—

either up front or when a situation happens—you may find yourself feeling unnecessary stress, or you might be tempted to succumb to the pressure and settle for a mediocre guy, or revert back to your old dating patterns and habits out of self-doubt or frustration.

By not trying to please everyone else, you get the chance to finally please yourself.

Your Internal Compass

Even the slightest internal nudges, butterfly sensations in your stomach, and faint whispers are trying to get your attention to remind you to *own your power*, to embrace it and see it as a good thing. Many people misinterpret *power* as being something bad or forceful. Accessing your power is about taking the time to find your way, to listen to your intuition, and to discover that you already have the answers.

You may not realize this, but you already possess an internal compass for creating outcomes—and it doesn't entail wishing on a star or praying for it to come true. I want to show you, not only how to discover a way to create the outcomes you want by using your internal compass, but also what gets in the way of owning your power.

Like I've been saying, real power is about taking the time to find your way, to listen to your guidance, and to discover your power. The little steps pave the way for taking bigger steps. It's going to be a lot about you having to experience managing your power.

As you step through the FOREVER Framework process, I suspect you'll experience feelings of uncertainty or fear of loneliness, despite having expanded your support network. Use any fear that comes up to fuel your continued forward progress.

FOREVER Feeling State

The FOREVER Feeling State can be used to identify and connect your thoughts and feelings—which links directly to your intuition. Think of intuition as an internal compass that's guiding you. It's a small, yet powerful, nudge that lets you know when something is off or wrong with someone else or a situation. Your intuition—what I like to refer to as your *FOREVER Feeling State*—helps to steer you in the right direction.

Shelly's first date with Keith was a little awkward. Between dinner and seeing the newest *Marvel* movie, they hung out at a video arcade connected to the theater. Keith was very attentive at dinner, but he seemed pretty distracted while Shelly played one of her favorite childhood games, Ms. Pac-Man. He excused himself to go use the restroom. When she'd finished her last round, Shelly headed toward the restrooms to wait for Keith. As she turned the corner, she saw him having a heated conversation with another woman. When she walked closer she heard the woman cursing and Keith apologizing for not calling her back.

Shelly's gut instantly felt knotted up. When the woman noticed Shelly walking up, she angrily darted away. When Shelly asked Keith what that was all about, he said it was his buddy's sister, and she was just mad at him because he hadn't returned the charcoal grill he'd borrowed from her for a tailgate party at the last Green Bay Packers home game. Wanting to give Keith the benefit of the doubt, Shelly tried to shrug it off, but her gut remained in knots the rest of the night. Over the next few weeks while Shelly and Keith were out on dates or hanging out that same sensation returned. It was progressively getting stronger, and she realized she couldn't ignore it anymore.

The Challenge

The biggest challenge most people have is with how to decode the messages or attach meaning to them. The truth, however, is simple. Those who struggle simply don't want to know what their FOREVER Feeling State is telling them. Their preference is to ignore the sensations they're feeling and let their minds create new meanings.

In Shelly's case, she wanted to give Keith the benefit of the doubt on their first date and believe his explanation. She liked Keith and thought he was a pretty good prospect, and she hoped he'd become a long-term boyfriend. But as time went on and they spent more time together, Shelly's body—*her gut*—was telling her that Keith was not a good fit.

Tuning In

To strengthen your intuition muscle, it's important to practice tuning in to what's going on within you as you continue through the steps. Notice how you are feeling—calm, excited, nervous, uneasy. Is your date congruent—are his words and actions matching? Do you have a sensation in your stomach (butterflies, a knot, or a pain)? Or is it like a lump in your throat, a tightness in your chest or in your back? Or do you have a sensation that your skin is crawling? These are internal alerts letting you know vital information about the other person. They are designed to keep you safe from emotional or physical harm. It's the fight or flight response.

This tool can be easily drawn out on a piece of paper, but I like to encourage my clients to visualize it in their minds so they can use it at any time. Envision a horizontal line scale with numbers ranging from -5 to +5, with a zero in the middle. Connecting how you're feeling to a number on the scale will help you quickly and easily decode what your body is trying to tell you.

As you begin to meet people, both online and for in-person dates, stay connected to what you're observing from the other person, as well as how you're feeling. As you begin dating again, you should always be in the positive zones.

When you learn how to step into your power and trust your intuition, the dating strategies and tactics that you'll be learning in the upcoming chapters will feel more natural and not icky or robotic.

Chapter 4

Step 3: Review and Reset

*I*n order to move forward in finding your Mr. Right, take some time to reflect on where you've been. Looking back will enable you to identify old patterns, so you don't repeat them again and so you can go in a new direction. With that information in hand, you can decide how you want to reset your trajectory from here.

Taking a deep dive into your past relationship history enables you to look toward the future—the one you've already identified that you want to create—with fresh eyes. As you look back you may be surprised by how little you settled for in the past. The beauty of this step is the newfound clarity you will possess about what you truly want, as well as what dating protocols and standards to adopt.

Let's Review Your Relationship Journey

Not having found your Mr. Right yet can indeed feel frustrating. Looking back at your overall relationship journey is a way to see where you've been and what wrong turns you may have taken, so you can change course.

To begin with, I ask clients to provide me with their relationship history. You can jot this down on paper. Begin with the most recent date or relationship listed first and then list all previous men back as far as you can come up with—ideally in chronological order. This list should include both casual and serious relationships, all of those things you appreciated, and the things you disliked.

For each name listed, include:

- Length of relationship (days, weeks, months or years) and the approximate dates when it started and ended.
- Did you have sex and, if so, how soon?
- Who ended the dating/relationship, and why?

- Do you still have a connection or friendship with this person? If so, explain.
- A brief back-story of each individual—marital status (for example, single and never married, or divorced and their total number of marriages), family of origin, job/ employment status, hobbies, and any other key factors, such as whether they have kids, if they travel for work, if they live nearby or a distance away, etc.

List up to twelve pros and twelve cons about each person listed—their personality, characteristics, lifestyle choices, personal preferences, attitude and behaviors, etc.

The pros list can contain characteristics you enjoyed and appreciated, and things you admired about each of your past relationships. The cons are the behaviors and aspects that you did *not* like and that you want to avoid as you go forward. There may even be things on your cons list that you now feel are absolute deal breakers.

Jot down everything you can remember, and then set it aside for a while. What you'll likely discover is while you are busy doing other things, your mind may still be mining the deepest recesses of your memory for more details. Also, feel free to tap into the memory banks of your trusted family and friends to see what they remember about your dating history.

What's Missing

Take some time to revisit your pros and cons list. Think about what things were missing in your past relationships. What can you see now that you may have missed before?

Were they *missing* any key ingredients that are important to you, such as:

- having shared interests
- working similar schedules
- living near one another
- similar education level
- similar political stance
- aligned religious or cultural beliefs
- tolerance of others who were different
- spending enough time together
- similar parenting styles
- creativity
- innovative/problem solver
- emotional maturity

Having clarity about these additional details allows you to stay connected to that vision of what you truly want in your Mr. Right.

Once these lists are completed, I have my clients email it to me so I can review it in advance of our next session. If you're doing this on your own, you can share your lists with a trusted friend and ask them to help you identify patterns in your relationship history.

Take a Field Trip

Amelia was invited to her friend's birthday celebration. The plans were for the group to meet for dinner and then hit the club scene downtown for the night. She was on a *dating break* but was worried about going out, because she didn't want to get hit on by random guys. I encouraged Amelia to go and suggested she wear a ring on her wedding finger and also pre-arrange with one of the guys in the group to hang closer to her for the night. That would give the illusion to the single guys that she was "taken," and so she could observe the behavior of the men at the various stops—what things she liked and disliked.

Amelia was in luck. She had her grandmother's antique wedding ring and her gay friend, Michael, was up for being her pretend boyfriend for the night.

Over the course of the evening, Amelia was able to observe the room and watch the guys' behaviors more objectively. She watched what the men did, noticed how they carried themselves, where their focus was, and who, if anyone, they were checking out. Within no time at all, she could tell which guys were single, coupled off, or married.

She made mental notes of physical features she was attracted to and how the men who were coupled off treated their lady. Amelia soon realized that she wanted to be with a man who treated her respectfully and like she was the only woman in the room.

Create Your Mr. Right Profile

In the step of *Futurizing Your Success*, you took some time to dream about Mr. Right and what he might be like. Now, in this step, reflecting back on your past relationship journey will help you formulate a partner profile for your Mr. Right.

In addition to past relationships you've been in, consider the other men you know personally—friends, in-laws, relatives, coworkers, business colleagues, and neighbors—and make note of the qualities these men possess that you'd like to have in a future relationship partner.

The positive qualities you identify in your past relationships, and in other men whom you know personally and admire, are what will inform your Mr. Right Profile.

I invite you to tune in to how you *feel* as you read through your Mr. Right Profile. How does being in that positive headspace feel? Do you feel more optimistic?

Envision yourself in a relationship with your dream partner and answer these questions:

- How are you carrying yourself?
- What does your life look like?
- What do you do in your free time?
- Imagine you're out for dinner together: What kind of drink do you order?
- What types of conversations do the two of you have? What topics do you discuss? What things do you share together? (Eavesdrop on one of those future conversations…. What do you hear?)
- What things do the two of you enjoy doing together?
- What else would you want for your life then?

Take some time to really imagine your future relationship and to anchor to it. Doing so will enable you to stay focused on what you truly want and deserve, and it will reduce the chance of you falling prey to another "waste of time" type.

It's Time to Reset

Resetting is about tossing out those old, unsuccessful dating patterns and habits and then starting anew. It's about embracing your internal knowing that this is what you want and then fully stepping into your power. From this place of owning your power, you're ready to uplevel your dating strategies, and to adopt new standards and protocols that will greatly increase your chances of finding your forever love sooner.

The chances of you finding your Mr. Right sooner will be greatly increased if you develop some pre-date protocols and standards for yourself. Below are some key steps to consider before you step back into the dating arena again.

Don't Try to be Someone You're Not

This is so simple, but with dating and trying to impress the other person, it can be easy to forget. If you're a 50-something Baby-boomer, don't try to be a Gen-Xer. If you're a 40-something Gen-Xer, don't try to be a 30-something hipster type. For God's sake, please do not even try to act like a Millennial, unless you are one! You will save yourself a lot of precious time and unnecessary grief if you will just be yourself, fully and unapologetically.

Subscribe to Reputable and Paid Dating Sites

When you're stepping back into the dating arena, it may seem tempting to jump on as many sites as possible to raise your chances of finding your forever love. But you need to know that not all sites are the right fit.

If you want a high-quality man, then why not invest in yourself and your future? I'm not a fan of free dating sites or apps, as they rarely produce high-quality prospects or tend to be for more shallow people who are usually only interested in a hook-up. Rather, I'd recommend subscribing to one paid dating site at a time for 3 to 6 months and focusing your energy and attention there. Dating and finding your Mr. Right is more of a marathon than a sprint, so be patient.

The truth is when you go for quantity over quality you end up struggling with trying to manage all the attention. It's easy to develop an unhealthy pattern of needing to receive regular recognition and then run the risk of being focused on other people paying attention to you—it becomes like a dopamine hit and can become addicting.

Update Your Dating Profile

Review the dating sites suggestions and recommendations for writing your profile. Match.com and eHarmony allow you to write a longer profile bio, whereas the dating apps tend to limit you to less than 500 characters. Whatever option you take, just be clear, concise, and honest. If you despise football, but love the creative arts, then be sure to share that important tidbit.

Do Your Due Diligence

When you meet someone online their last name may be intentionally left off the dating site, or they're able to use a pseudonym or avatar name. Once you've had a chance to chat with someone online, and then on the phone, find out their last name. This is your opportunity to do some online research to see who this person is.

You can search for his social media profiles (Facebook, Twitter, Instagram, LinkedIn, Snapchat, etc.) to see what you can find. If he's not on social media, then I'd be wary of proceeding forward with any level of communication. *(Unless he's got a legit reason, like he works for the CIA! LOL!)* You should also check the state court system to see if or what legal issues he may have had. If he's divorced, that should be listed. You can certainly check other states as well if he's lived elsewhere that you know of.

Also, don't hesitate to find out who you might know in common, and then don't be afraid to ask your mutual acquaintance about your potential date—who he is, his background, etc. If you want to get to know the guy faster, act like a true detective…. You won't regret it.

Be Socially Mindful

Having your life on display can be fun, and it's also a great way to stay connected with friends and loved ones. But know that over-sharing and over-posting can get out of hand. Be mindful not to air your dirty laundry about feeling lonely or that you just got dumped…again. It's usually easy to see when others are using social media to solicit sympathy or attention. I would also recommend you not post about every date you go on, as that will only entice your friends and followers to question you unnecessarily. Save that for when you've found your Mr. Right and want to share your happiness with your friends and followers.

Dress for Success

I don't mean that you wear corporate attire out on a date, nor do I mean you should dress provocatively. Sure, some guys might enjoy seeing your cleavage, but in all honestly, it makes you look more desperate or gives off the vibe that you're just a piece of ass. What's most important is that you put forethought and energy into your date night outfits. You'll feel much more confident if you're wearing clothes (and shoes) that are comfortable and work with your body type. Know, too, that not all trending styles look good on every body. Practice sitting down to be sure the material isn't too tight fitting, and take a few laps around the shoe store with the new pair of shoes you've been drooling over, before you buy them. The worst is wearing an outfit that's too tight or constricting and shoes that kill your feet after 10 minutes. Also, be sure you have a few outfits in the event you go on multiple dates with the same person. I find that having tops and bottoms that are easily interchangeable give you the most mileage. So, take some time to pre-plan your date night outfits.

Meet Your Date Out

I recommend that you arrive separately when you meet your date in-person for the first time, and even for the first few dates.

You can drive yourself, take the bus, or call an Uber or Lyft. It's standard protocol today that your date not know exactly where you live. He needs to earn the right and privilege of knowing where you live and being able to pick you up at your house, and only if he meets your pre-set criteria.

If you're nervous and feeling uncertain, and want to feel more secure on your first date, don't hesitate to invite your friends to be present for the evening. This should be done discreetly, and you should not engage with them in front of your date. Save the updates for when you need to use the bathroom or for the next day.

If you go alone, always be sure to let a friend or loved one know that you have a date and where you'll be going for the evening.

Keep It Classy

A key to finding your Mr. Right is to make sure you're staying in control. Make it a rule of thumb not to get drunk or even tipsy on a date. You want to be fully prepared for anything that can happen on a date, so know your limits. If martinis are your nemesis, then opt for a wine spritzer or a seltzer water instead. Alcohol can greatly impair your judgment and your ability to stay in control. Too much alcohol can make even the dumpster diving bum behind the night club look sexy! Plus, nobody *really* enjoys doing the "walk (or drive) of shame" back home the next morning, or worse, trying to figure out how to get last night's drunken regret out of your bed and out the door. Staying sober also enables your mind to function with more clarity.

Take the Edge Off

Sally regretted sleeping with a guy on her first date. She'd been longing for the full-body rush that comes from an orgasm. She found that when she'd go out and meet an attractive man at the clubs, she could easily succumb to any sexual advances. During our coaching session I invited Sally to get herself a new vibrator to take the edge off before she goes on a date. Sally tried it before her next date and found that her mind was more clear, and she could tune into the important stuff—like whether or not her date matched the characteristics she was looking for in a future relationship partner.

I am a firm believer in keeping your wits about you when you're on a date or even out with your friends for a fun evening. When you step back into the dating arena, it can be very tempting to *not* stay in control, let yourself be seduced by some sexy-eyes guy, and end up making the mistake of sleeping with him on the first date. You're especially vulnerable if you've not had sex in a while. Therefore, I suggest to all of my clients to get themselves off before they go on a date. This might be a surprising recommendation, but I promise you it definitely takes the edge off and enables you to stay focused. You can order devices online, from a Pure Romance party consultant, or you can visit your local adult toy store to peruse their inventory. The benefit of going to a store is you can talk to the staff, get recommendations, and actually open the box to look at the items before buying. You don't have to go all crazy and get some wild contraption or spend a lot of money... something simple will usually do the trick!

The Prize Never Chases

We live in an era where women are very independent and capable of taking care of themselves and are in charge. Thanks in part to societal changes and expectations, and the media—reality TV, magazines, online articles, and the like—women have shifted far away from letting a man, or even expecting him, to *court* her (even though deep down that's what we really want). And that has led women to take on the role more often as the pursuer versus allowing the man to actually do more of the heavy lifting.

Instead, women often take the lead in pursing men, be it by swiping right, liking a profile, instigating online conversations, asking for his phone number, or even walking up to a guy and letting him know directly (verbally or with a certain look) that she's into him. Sure, guys definitely like this, but know that they don't necessarily view those actions as "long-term committed relationship" potential.

This might sound old-fashioned or out of touch with reality, but the truth is, ladies, if you're looking to finally find your forever man, then you will need to chill on the excessive assertiveness a bit—and for sure stop behaving like you're some sex kitten who'll drop to her knees to try to win him over. You can save all that adventurous play for when you know he's a keeper.

The truth is, when it comes to relationships, the female is *the prize*. I don't mean this in any degrading or disrespectful manner. Rather, when you look at animals in nature, it's *typically* the male who pursues or tries to persuade the female to be his partner. The same nature applies to humans—it's the female who then decides if she's going to accept the male.

Obviously, there are some men who don't want to do any of the work and prefer for the female to chase them. These tend to be the narcissists, the emotionally immature, the commitment-phobes, the playboys, or those who only want to use you for sex.

Variety is the Spice of Life

The nice thing about stepping back into the dating arena is that you get the opportunity to go on a variety of different types of dates. If you look at dating as a time to have fun and explore getting to know another person versus treating it like a chore, you will drastically increase your chances of finding your future partner sooner.

I personally feel that the more variety you let yourself experience, be it the types of dates or men, the better! Who wants to always only go on a *dinner and a movie* date? They're great if you want to try out a new restaurant or introduce your date to your favorite eatery, or see the latest new release, but doing the *same ole thing* can get pretty boring. Plus, if all you do are the standard kind of dates, then I think you're missing out on having some real fun, staying connected with yourself and what brings you joy, and more importantly getting to see your date in action in different scenarios. Whether you enjoy traditional, adventurous, romantic, or fun-themed dates, simply being open to adding variety to your dates can enable you to see quicker if your date aligns with you and what you enjoy and want in life.

For an extensive list of date theme ideas, go to www.findingforeverlovebook.com to download the *Finding Forever Love Tool Kit*.

The best part about dating is that you get to expand your experiences and continue to add to and subtract from those things you're looking for in a future relationship partner. Keep in mind that even a mediocre man can introduce you to new things you never expected or considered, so why not let yourself play and embrace this time.

Review your past relationship history. Identify the negative patterns and consider positive characteristics from that history. You will see more clearly what you want in a future relationship partner. Prior to that date, learn what resources and techniques you can use. You will better focus on your date and be mentally present for the overall experience.

In the next chapter, we will look at what to do to maximize the evaluation opportunity available during the date itself.

Chapter 5
Step 4: Evaluate Your Date

*E*valuating your date will help you step into your power fully, uncover your voice, and begin to see the life you want for yourself in real time. When you return to dating it's good to think in advance about what you want to get out of the conversation, and that starts by knowing what to ask and why.

Your goal is to really set yourself up for success by being able to discern whether the guy in front of you is a fit for you or not, and if so, to build on what you know is actually working. Then honor your style by asking questions. Step into your power and ask them in the way you know works best for you.

Staying Calm

Talk to any single ladies, and you're bound to hear all sorts of dating horror stories. Heck, I could write another book just on that topic! Putting yourself out there does make you vulnerable, but know that it doesn't mean you need to be paranoid and let your mind run rampant with crazy "what if" scenarios. Refrain from listening to any girlfriends who tend to only date high drama guys, playboys, or all-around crazy men.

Nor should you listen to your clueless mother who hasn't dated in 40 years but saw an episode of Dr. Phil and is freaked out you're going to get mugged, roofied, and raped, or even killed. Yeah, let's not slip down that rabbit hole! If you know how to tap into and trust your intuition, and you're smart about things, you should be okay.

Create a Date Scorecard

More times than not, singles try to keep a mental scorecard of the different people they meet online, are seeing, or have dated. They think they can keep track of everything, but in truth it's really easy to ignore certain details or forget to ask early on. They think writing it down is more of a chore, or maybe that there's something wrong with actually keeping track. But I disagree.

Just as it's important to know what you want in a future relationship partner, it's also just as important to be able to clearly *see* the person before you in order to be able to size them up. Given the abundance of dating sites and apps available now, it can be hard to keep track of the details of each person you're chatting with.

The scorecard contains all of the "must have's" that you're looking for, as well as having space for jotting down their back-story, any inconsistent information, red flags, or deal breakers. My clients greatly benefit from keeping a running log (or journal) about each of their dates to help them better identify if he's a potential fit or not.

Getting Acquainted

Getting to know someone new is always interesting. Some people are nervous, others are shy and not very forthcoming with information, while others can over-share, act arrogant, or come on way too strong or serious (the "Hi, let's get married!" quick-draw type).

You've got your classic introverts and extroverts, and those who fall along the broad spectrum between the two extremes. But the only way to start to get to know someone is to actually talk with them on the phone, video chat, or in-person.

Email, texting, and instant messaging don't necessarily count for really getting to know someone, because it's easy to hide behind technology and pretend to be something or someone you're not. It's vital to be able to utilize as many of your senses as you can, so you can read between the words where the truth lies.

In addition, there are some people who simply don't know how to express themselves through written communication. The only upside is you'll be able to tell if the other person knows how to spell or construct a complete sentence.

The goal of getting to know someone is to find out if they fit what you're looking for. And to do that you have to be willing and able to come out of your shell, and find out the key information that you need and want to know.

Translating Circumstances

You may not instantly become some *eagle eye* who can spot the BS from a mile away. But as more time goes on you want to feel as if you can see it like a wet footprint, so you can make your evaluations from a place of integrity, and a place of detachment.

It's about using your skills of perception—"*the process of integrating, organizing, and interpreting sensations*"—which works hand-in-hand with your intuition to be able to translate his stories and circumstances.

Is what he's saying to you completely honest, or is it more fluff and trying to "sell" himself to you? It's about learning how to spot it and be able to cut through any BS.

You can translate stories by learning how to tap into your five senses.

- **See**—Watch their body language.
- **Hear**—Listen to all they're saying: tone of voice, word choice, topic patterns (is it all about them?).
- **Touch**—Feel the sensation you get in your stomach. That's your intuition. Or physically—when they touch you. For example, when they hug you, does it feels cold or insincere? Is their handshake overpowering?
- **Smell**—Does something "smell" wrong? Does something seem odd? Is there an incongruence between his words and actions?
- **Taste**—Drink in the encounter. If it gives you a bad taste in your mouth, it could be reminding you of an unpleasant memory.

Breadcrumbing

Breadcrumbing is all about slowly sharing bits and pieces about yourself and your life. You may have heard the saying: "How do you eat an elephant? One bite at a time." Well, it's similar in the beginning with dating in that you only want to share small spoonfuls at a time. This is important so as to keep yourself more in control of the situation. You don't want to reveal too much too soon. It's not about being coy, rather it's about being smart and keeping your guard up or until he's earned the right to know more intimate details about you.

When you do share about yourself, be fully and clearly you, and don't fake it. Don't pretend to be anyone other than who you actually are. The fact is that there are going to be some people who meet you in person and just won't like you. And, there's going to be people who don't fit with what you ultimately want, and you'll have to cut them loose and let that go.

Getting Through the Small Talk

First dates can be pretty awkward, even if you've already gotten acquainted over the phone. Know that finally seeing the "in real life" person you've been talking to can stir up some emotional reactions—both good and bad—that may take some time to settle into.

Starting out with small talk is an excellent way to ease into learning and sharing more information with one another. If a guy seems to have a hard time talking, don't be afraid to guide the conversation until you get to a topic where he feels more comfortable.

Let Him Show You Who He Really Is

If your date pulls the classic faux pas and shares all about his ex or complains how he got crapped on, ripped off, or screwed over—don't interrupt, just sit back and listen—let him talk.

This is where you get to learn more about who this guy really is. If you know what to listen for and how to trust your intuition, this is the perfect opportunity to learn who he *really* is.

In some situations when a guy pukes out all his troubles, it's typically because he's still reeling from the last experience. It feels good to have someone new who'll listen and possibly feel sorry for him. The men I've coached admit this has happened for them when they hopped back into the dating arena right away in hopes of getting over their ex.

There are other situations where the guy is just nervous and didn't know what else to talk about beyond the weather or sports, so he just starts yammering on about himself and out comes the "ex" stories. It happens.

Based on your experience interacting with these individuals, you should know where to draw the line. You can shift gears by simply saying: *"Wow, that's too bad. Well, I have a rule that I don't talk about my exes on dates. I find it kind of tacky. So with that, tell me more about yourself/your hobbies/your job."*

The "still reeling" guy may not get the hint and will just circle back to complaining, or he may get defensive. The nervous guy will likely apologize for being rude and move on to answering your question.

Please know that there are guys out there who prey on women who seem naïve or who are strong caretaker types. These women are attractive because they tend to easily fall for the sob story and try to "out-do" the ex who crapped on this "great guy." In reality, these guys are the ones who usually drop the "great guy" act and soon treat their lady like garbage, and then act all wounded later when they get dumped or left. If at all possible, don't get sucked into that vortex of feeling sorry for them.

Stealth Questioning

Many women do not know what all to look for in order to find their Mr. Right. It takes knowing what and how to ask the right questions.

Some people are afraid to ask questions because they don't want to come off like they're interviewing their date. They instead want to seem "cool" and try to keep things casual and pretend they're okay with not knowing, so as to avoid freaking out the prospect or date and scaring them away. I get that you don't want to come across as interrogating, but at the same time I don't really buy it. Not asking questions and pretending you're cool with *whatever* is really just a way to delay knowing the truth about the other person. It's also an easy way to delay or distract yourself from your goal of finding your forever love sooner.

As I mentioned earlier on, when you know upfront what you want in a future partner, then it's easier to know what questions to ask and when, so you're not wasting your time.

The way to ask questions and stay under the radar is to be stealthy about it and to simply have conversations and let him talk. Now, this is no dis on men, but quite honestly, most men love to talk about themselves. Early on they're typically on their best behavior and want to say all the right things that will impress you. So, you may not learn the real story right away, but in no time you *can*, simply by paying attention.

You start by asking some general "get to know you" questions, and from there you dig a little deeper each time you talk, to learn more. In the midst of your conversations and asking your stealthy questions, you should also share things about your life too that complement the conversation topic. Because let's face it, he's ultimately trying to figure out if you're a potential keeper or just a fling.

There are tons of questions you can ask as you're getting acquainted with someone, and this link will take you to a list of my all-time favorites. For a checklist of must-ask questions, go to www.findingforeverlovebook.com to download the *Finding Forever Love Tool Kit*.

You can decide which questions you want to ask, to whom, and when, based on what feels right in the moment. The list of questions can also be used as key points to listen for during conversations to help you determine if the guy is a potential fit or not.

What to Listen For

When dating, listening is more important than talking. It enables you to better see a man's true character. You learn a great deal about a person when you let them talk and share their stories. This happens over the course of weeks and months, and if he ends up being a keeper, you'll continue to learn about him for years to come.

Initially, find out about his work, kids (if any), family, and education. As times goes on, you'll get to learn more about his life experiences. As you listen, I encourage you to pay attention to what his tolerances and intolerances are. Where does he stand on issues that mean a lot to you, such as politics, the environment, religion, and more? Don't be afraid to ask him why he holds his particular stance or opinion. What is he passionate about?

In his stories, does he talk about how he's taken advantage of others, such as consistently charging full price for tickets for friends or loved ones when he got them at a discount? Does he seem more prone to or drawn to drama—at work, with family, or strangers? Does he have a propensity to self-sabotage, such as procrastinating achieving goals, or falling prey to buffers such as smoking, drinking, drugs, gambling, etc.?

As you tune into the depth and breadth of his life experiences, listen in to see if he mentions learning from his past mistakes. Listening for who he is will help you decide if and when to let your guard down more and share more in-depth information about your life.

As you meet different men, fill out your dating scorecard, and don't hesitate to compare them to your past dating experiences or relationships.

Cautions, Guardrails, and Deal Breakers

Knowing how to tap into and trust your intuition will help you spot things quicker that don't jibe with what makes you feel comfortable. This can include reading his body language, noticing if his words and actions don't match, watching how he behaves toward you on the date, observing how he treats others (servers, bartenders), checking in with yourself to feel whether he's too over the top for your liking, etc. In addition, if you get a bad vibe that he's kind of creepy, a narcissist, or just not your type, don't be afraid to cut your losses right there.

There's no shame in being honest and telling a guy, *"I appreciate meeting up with you tonight, but I have to be honest, I can't do this."* If you feel guilty, feel free to offer to pay the bill. The sooner you can make the decision to cut and run, the more relieved you'll feel that you're not wasting time with someone who doesn't fit what you want.

Use the FOREVER Feeling State Tool

Dating site algorithm or personality matches are helpful, but staying tuned into your FOREVER Feeling State is where the real magic happens.

It's tempting to want to give people the benefit of the doubt and ignore your gut. Rationale I've heard from clients over the years includes: letting your mind trick you into thinking that maybe your first impression was wrong, or thinking you can rescue them from their current situation or their past struggles, or you've got that deep nagging voice that says being with someone is better than having no one.

Remember that part of having self-respect is to also not fall prey to any dating games. They are ultimately a waste of your time. So, if it feels like a game—trust your gut—call it out and step away fast. Sticking around to try to help or fix will only leave you frustrated in the end.

The truth is this: Believe people the first time they show you who they really are—which means you then will need to take action.

Winners vs. Qualifiers

Maria was frustrated with dating and growing more impatient that she hadn't yet met her Mr. Right. She said, "Screw it, I don't need to keep punishing myself waiting to find the perfect man. I'm just going to make it work with Craig, he's nice enough to me." That was at a time when Maria was feeling exhausted from dating guys who only met some of her criteria. Craig was a nice guy and had qualities Maria liked, but he lacked those key characteristics she'd dreamed of having in a forever partner. She was afraid she might never find her Mr. Right and was on the verge of settling.

What Maria didn't fully understand at the time was the difference between "qualifiers" and "winners." Qualifiers meet our basic needs—they're more the mediocre guys that many women settle for. They lack that "wow factor" that differentiates them from the rest.

Whereas winners go above and beyond—these are the men who have depth and substance. The "wow factor" that winners possess can be visible or perceived—they stand out in a different and unique way than anyone else you've met before.

After some coaching, Maria was able to see that she was out of Craig's league and by continuing to date him, she was really just settling.

I want you to understand how totally doable finding your Mr. Right is.

~~~~~~

Learning how to evaluate your date and utilizing the FOREVER Feeling State tool will help you find the best dating prospects.

In the next chapter, we'll talk about how to stay true to your values and your future goal of finding your Mr. Right.

Chapter 6

Step 5: Value Your Vision

*I*n the previous chapters you've envisioned your dream relationship partner and learned ways to evaluate your date, as well as other things to consider incorporating into your new dating strategy.

This step is about keeping you connected to your vision by addressing challenges that can arise—and potentially throw you off course—as you journey to finding your forever love.

Shiny Object Syndrome

What emotionally healthy women and men want in a relationship is truly the same at the core—love, connection, security, respect, and happiness. But given the world we live in today, that can be easily forgotten. Our society is addicted to instant gratification. We're bombarded with reality TV shows that showcase superficial women who act like spoiled divas and relish in instigating drama. With the advent of social media, so many live behind a false happiness persona. All of this makes dating challenging, because we can get unconsciously sucked into thinking the superficial stuff is more important than our core desires.

Staying focused on your goal of finding your Mr. Right is key. It's about staying on your own side while you keep evaluating your date, even when you feel vulnerable. It's about trusting your evaluations versus getting blinded by some "shiny object man" sitting in front of you. Paying attention enables you to watch for key indicators of what may or may not be a fit for what you're looking for in your Mr. Right.

When Fear Shows Up

The biggest fear is: *What if this doesn't work?* And then I'm going to be sitting here feeling like a loser. Well, my dear, we're going to do everything in our power for that not to happen.

You may get over the initial fear of putting yourself out there again, but the fear never goes away fully. It can raise its head again and start saying: *What if I can't make this happen? What if I can't do this? Who am I to be so selective or picky?* All of those questions and fears are common.

When fear shows up, it will help to get centered again by controlling your body's respiration rate and relaxing any muscle tension. You can do this in a variety of ways, but my favorite is to find a quiet place to lie down. Or if you can't lie down, find a comfortable place to sit with your feet planted on the ground.

Lay down on the floor or a bed where your whole backside has contact with the surface. In yoga this is referred to as the dead man's pose. Close your eyes and begin to focus on your breathing, inhaling slowly in through your nose and out through your mouth. As you exhale, take your time and let your lungs empty as completely as you can. At first your breathing will likely be faster and shallower. Continue to focus on slowing your breaths, and take your time. As your breathing settles down, so will your heart rate.

As you're working at controlling your respiration rate, tune into your body. Are you feeling any muscle tightness? If so, focus your thoughts on each spot individually and breath into the tightness until is subsides. Then move to the next spot. Continue to do this until your body feels relaxed.

What tends to happen during this re-centering exercise is your once-anxious mind, has stopped buzzing with all those fearful questions. But, if you have trouble getting back to center, you can also listen to guided meditations to help you relax and step away from fearful thoughts.

It's important that you accept that fear will return from time to time. But more so, that you are kind to yourself when it happens, while still moving forward.

Introducing Your Kids

There are varying opinions on when and if to introduce your kids to your dates, if at all.

In the beginning, I wasn't too keen on the idea of an early introduction, because I didn't want to confuse my kids or scare off my date. But after I had been in a couple relationships, I changed my approach and introduced my kids very early on when dating a new guy. I had learned the hard way that two different boyfriends had felt uncomfortable with my boys. The first one didn't have boys, he had girls, and had no idea how to "parent boys." And the other guy had a son who was only 3 years old, and he couldn't relate to my kids being in middle and high school at the time.

My kids could sense that these guys didn't really care for them—and knew how to push their buttons—but because I'd felt somewhat invested in each of those separate relationships, it caused friction between my boys and me.

After realizing that, I shifted gears and introduced my boys to my new date, usually by the third or fourth date (if he met my initial criteria and advanced to being able to pick me up for a date at my house for the first time). My boys turned out to be great judges of character, which helped me weed out a few "waste of time" guys early on, which was nice!

In reality, you need to do what you feel is best based on your situation. But I feel it's okay to toss out the notion that you must keep your date away from your home life until you've invested a bunch of time. Base your decision about when or if to set up an introduction on your intuition and the FOREVER Feeling State. Being honest and upfront with your kids that you are dating and letting them get used to meeting your dates is by no means detrimental to their health or well-being. It's an opportunity for your kids to learn that finding the ideal relationship partner takes trial and error.

It's also a great opportunity to see how the guy reacts and responds to your kids. You can invite your date to come over to your house to meet your kids, or you can have him meet you all for the first time in a more neutral setting. If he's not interested in meeting your kids, then the writing is on the wall—he's most likely not Mr. Right potential.

In my case, my kids were older and knew I was actively dating. I wanted to be darn sure up-front the guy who was potentially looking for a long-term relationship was open and accepting of my kids—because we were a package deal.

Let's Talk About Sex

Sex is something that some women may not even really consider when it comes down to deciding if a man is *keeper* material. What I've heard from countless women over the years is: *"just as long as he's not into weird kinky stuff, I'm fine."* But when I asked them to be more specific about what they meant, they weren't always able to articulate it. But since the *Fifty Shades of Grey* book series came out, that's when I got more clarification. They'd love the gorgeous billionaire part, but were not all that crazy about the S&M sex stuff.

If I had a dollar for every expert opinion on the right amount of time to wait, I swear I'd be rich! One theory in particular I read—in one of Steve Harvey's books years ago—suggested waiting three months to ensure the guy is serious about you. Conceptually, that might sound okay, but is it realistic? Do you really want to invest 90 whole days before you find out how he might be in the sack?

Candi had been friends with Ben for a couple years. He'd never been married before and had only had a few relationships. Ben made her laugh, and Candi enjoyed hanging out with him when she was between relationships—happy hour after work, watching 4th of July fireworks together, and attending a music festival.

One night after attending a haunted house together near Ben's place, he invited Candi over to his apartment for the first time. They enjoyed a few drinks while they talked, and he showed her his various collections. Candi wasn't necessarily physically attracted to Ben, but she did feel an emotional connection. Feeling curious about what it would be like to kiss him, she leaned in, and in mere minutes they were in the throes of having sex on his couch. Ben was an okay kisser, but the sex was horrible. Candi was shocked, but pretended everything was fine. She didn't have the courage to tell Ben the truth, so she decided to avoid him for a while saying she was busy with work.

Feeling guilty for how she behaved, and also second-guessing that maybe it was the wine or the couch to blame, Candi decided to give it another shot a couple months later. This time was no different—sex was awful again—but this time she couldn't hide it from Ben. Over those few years, unbeknownst to Candi, Ben had fallen in love with her. When she finally told him what was wrong and that this wasn't going to work for her, Ben was devastated and felt extremely embarrassed. Candi felt horrible too because she cared about Ben, but she also knew that having great sex was very important to her. She wasn't willing to settle, nor should she have.

How Long to Wait

If you want to set your own rule for "x" number of months, that's certainly your choice, but my only caution is to not wait too long where you're so emotionally connected, like Candi, and then you have sex and it totally sucks. You may have the belief that if you love each other that then sex will be great, regardless. Well, that might be true, but then again it could end up disappointing.

Whatever your beliefs are about sex—what you like or don't like, what you're open to or adamantly opposed to—it's important to factor that into the equation. Being able to talk to your potential future partner about what's important to you, what you're interested in possibly exploring, as well as what your "hell no's" are beforehand will help you determine if you even want to take that next step with him.

What *I* personally believe in is *not* sleeping with the guy right away. This comes from personal experience and falsely thinking sex is how you get a guy to like you. It's not! If at all possible, give yourself a month to get to know him better. Even if it feels right, take a pause and ask yourself if you're ready to explore having sex with this guy. Waiting is also about getting the respect you deserve, and an emotionally mature man will respect your wish to wait. You also get the ultimate prize of maintaining your dignity and self-esteem while earning the respect of the man who recognizes that you *are* worth the wait.

The other thing I feel strongly about is that you talk about sex with him before you have sex with him. Don't just "let it happen." If you want it to feel special, plan when it will happen. I understand it might feel uncomfortable or awkward, but how he talks with you about sex will also help you get to know him more intimately. If he talks like he can't wait to *get you into bed*—versus wanting to connect intimately and create a deeper bond in your relationship—then he's probably not long-term relationship material.

Managing Drama

The biggest thing that has come up for my clients going through the FOREVER Framework is drama, and getting in their own way. Drama can show up in a variety of ways, and knowing what it can look like will help you see it more objectively so that you can best manage it.

In the past, you may have been drawn to the drama versus the calm. The drama is where things feel exciting, but in reality, it just leads to unneeded stress and frustration. People who can't break away from high-drama types tend to be those who also don't want to take any responsibility for their life. Be mindful of self-sabotage—where things are so good you need to blow things up because, ironically, having it so good is too uncomfortable. Know that there's more opportunity with calm, no-drama relationships.

Being resilient when challenges arise is key to keeping you on your path to success and finding your Mr. Right. It enables you to roll with whatever comes your way. But it takes a lot of time and effort when you attempt to go at it by yourself. Until you unlock this skillset within yourself, finding and using your ability to not allow unexpected drama to knock you off course will be more challenging. And until you realize how you might continue to be drawn to drama, you will not attract a man worthy to have *you* in his life.

The truth is this: staying true to your vision and what you want in a future relationship partner *opens you up* to new opportunities, and you're able to get to know yourself better. Being able to hold onto that while stepping back into dating again can be a tricky balancing act.

Drama will come up at different times and in different ways, some of which I've already shared in this chapter. What's important is that, if you find yourself stumbling or you get knocked off track, that you don't choose to give up or quit. Challenges arise to test your commitment to continue to evolve into the woman who is ready to welcome her forever love.

The Deciding Factor

First, let me share one secret about being able to make a decision that is aligned and authentic: Your heart must be open, soft, and yes, even vulnerable. You make this happen by letting down your guard and bringing all of you to the relationship.

Staying self-aware and continuing to be able to revel in what delights you—that is your own personal imprint of joy. It awakens your power, your heart, and your awareness of your preferences. And that's why you need to also allow yourself to be vulnerable.

Being able to accelerate your decision-making is a key piece to having relationship success sooner. It's not about pushing and forcing. As you've learned, it's about tapping into your intuition, and understanding what you really, truly want in your forever love.

If you get lost because you ignored your preferences or stuffed them down for so long that you don't even know what you like anymore, then it may be a challenge to access your intuition at first. Your intuition needs you to trust yourself in order to be able to know yourself. Knowing yourself is about allowing yourself to want what you want, unapologetically.

Delight in the preferences of your heart—they teach you how to set your intentions and how to make a wise decision.

~~~~~~

With your vision identified and in clear focus, now you are ready to step into the life, romantic and otherwise, that takes you into the vision you want to live.

Chapter 1

Step 6: Establish Your Independence

*n*early every marriage expert has uttered the phrase: "You have to make your relationship top priority if you want it to be successful." The problem with many women in a new relationship is they do just that. They place the importance of being in a relationship above everything else in their life. They blindly slip into (or continue learned habits in) the roles of caretakers and people-pleasers. It's like they fall into quicksand and forget who they are and that they are a priority.

If you've been in or exposed to unhealthy or abusive relationships before, you've probably experienced some degree of codependency—either habitual behaviors or thinking, or both—and struggled with retaining your independence. This chapter takes a side-step to look at codependency and how to prevent it from self-sabotaging a new relationship.

Antidote for Codependency

Establishing your independence is the antidote to unknowingly slipping into codependent behaviors. Maintaining your independence—your individual identity—has a healthy place in a relationship.

As relationships intensify and integrate, it's easy to be more "attached at the hip" as you grow into a more bonded stage. It's important to allow yourself to continue to grow and discover in who you are, both before and after you say "I do."

When you are dating, it's very easy to spend all of your available free time with your new boyfriend. This is part of the "coming together bonding" phase in relationships. What's key is that you don't get lost in being a couple and forget who you are.

If things in your life start to feel out of balance—and know that this isn't necessarily wrong or bad—you can do a U-turn by returning to more self-empowering actions or by adding in more "you time" space, again.

This also includes your thinking. Caring about someone does not automatically mean you must think about them constantly, anticipate their every need, be there for them at all times, or rescue them out of every difficult or challenging situation that comes up. Your job is not to be some overbearing controlling mother-type to your new relationship partner, nor is it their job to be yours. Allow your partner to figure things out, and let them learn how to ask for help if they feel they truly need it.

It is important to recharge yourself when you notice things have become lopsided and you're longing for a bit of independence. You can have that.

Using Your Voice

Overcoming codependency can start by simply giving yourself what you need—stepping through fear and stating or asking for what you need.

For example, if you have a project to work on or an exam to study for and you want some uninterrupted quiet time, tell your partner that's what you need. Be upfront and clear—do not assume he'll know what you mean or expect him to read your mind. And if necessary, don't hesitate to repeat your boundary and wishes should your boyfriend have a short-term memory lapse.

Or, if you want help with household chores, shuttling kids, solving a problem, etc., don't be afraid to ask for what you need. A suggested way to ask for help might be: "I have to get Jane to dance practice, but I've got a late meeting at work that day. If you're available, would you be able to help me out?" But know that asking doesn't always mean you can or should expect an automatic "yes."

Your needs are important, and it's okay to talk about them. The same holds true with your partner. Remain open to hearing and respecting his needs, too.

Breaking up with Codependency

The challenging part about establishing your independence, while in a relationship, comes if you or your new partner have a codependent history with past relationships. Those who struggle with codependency may feel guilty about doing nurturing things for themselves or always putting others before them.

Being able to spot codependent tendencies in your partner will enable you to encourage them to do those things that fill them with joy, challenge them, and even relieve stress. The key is to encourage but not force it.

Teach your partner by example how to break up with codependency by keeping girls night out dates, encouraging him to do things like going golfing with his buddies, going fishing, or pursuing (or picking back up) a hobby. When you come back together after your time apart, share your experiences with one another and be sincerely appreciative of the newfound energy you each have.

If you struggle with codependent tendencies, then know that you will likely have to work hard at stepping through that discomfort. Your partner does not have to be at your side constantly. It's important to be supportive of his passions and projects and allow yourself to pursue other interests, too.

Learn When to Pivot

What you've learned in the previous chapters is intended to help you find your Mr. Right sooner and prevent you from wasting your time. However, it's important to know that there can be unique circumstances that arise which may force you to shift gears, or pivot.

Connie was certain Brad was *the one*, and their relationship had been progressing forward. Everything seemed to align with what she wanted in a life partner and for her future. Brad was an assistant football coach at a college in the Midwest and loved his job. The year before they met, Brad had applied at other division one colleges around the U.S. The night of their six-month dating anniversary, Brad shared the news that he'd just been offered his dream job as a head football coach at Florida

State. Connie's heart dropped. She was happy for Brad, but there was no way she could move to be with him because of the ages of her kids and her custody agreement. The only option would be for Connie and Brad to have a long-distance relationship, but that seemed impossible with her demanding job and her kids' schedules.

Sometimes situations can arise that don't work with where your life is today and force you to re-think your relationship and future plans. Connie could have allowed this exciting and tough news to trigger codependent behaviors—panicky thoughts about losing Brad forever and consequently trying to make arrangements to change her custody agreement with the court, or decide to relinquish custody of her kids altogether to follow Brad to Florida.

Being realistic and honest with yourself is important, as well as being able to openly discuss it with your boyfriend. In Connie and Brad's situation, they agreed it was best for Brad to pursue his career goal and move away, because staying back would likely create resentment or worse, he'd feel like he was sacrificing his dreams due to Connie's current circumstances. They ultimately decided, instead of ending their relationship, to just see what happened, and allow one another to maintain their independence.

Learning to let go of self-sabotaging behaviors and be able to ask for what you need will help you have *healthier* relationships, so you are fully prepared to *embrace your forever love.*

In the next chapter, we'll discuss the final step of the FOREVER Framework process—what it looks like once you meet your Mr. Right and what life looks like on the other side of your search process.

Chapter 8
Step 7: Respect Reality

*I*n earlier chapters, you learned about futurizing your success, owning your power, creating dating protocols and standards, how to evaluate potential prospects, valuing your vision, and establishing your independence from codependent behaviors. The cool thing about being at this point is that you've already learned how to make many lasting changes in your life– which is something so many others only dream of doing for themselves.

Too often, women fantasize about some Prince Charming magically appearing on their doorstep to sweep them away. Sorry ladies… that's not going to happen!

If you do the work, you're going to get the "keys to the kingdom" when it comes to finding your forever love. In this chapter, we gear up for reality and what you can expect when you finally meet your Mr. Right.

You've Found a Keeper

A real man is someone who can help draw out your greatness more and whom you can also do the same for.

When you discover you've got a keeper, your life will shift in ways you've never imagined possible. The most frequently asked questions I get from clients and loved ones is *How do you know?* followed by *What does it feel like?* What I say, based on my personal experience, is that it's a knowing that you feel throughout your entire being.

There's a sense of calm and certainty from the beginning, and you already know that your relationship is going to go the distance. Many have described it as feeling like "coming home," where others refer to it as a "soul mate connection."

You're both on the same page—your wants, needs, goals, and dreams are similar—and your desire to be together is mutually strong. You feel like long-lost best friends who just "get" each other right away. Any flaws or shortcomings that may have been glaring in previous relationships, aren't even on your radar because you accept one another fully, and you deeply respect each other as unique and special individuals. You're both comfortable being completely yourselves and are not afraid to challenge and push one another to continue to grow and become your best selves. Things feel *easy*, like it's no work at all to be in this relationship. You'll be filled with *"Yes! Thank you! More, please!"* thoughts!

What Real Commitment Looks Like

Once you've met your Mr. Right, there are number of bonding phases you'll go through– some may happen swifter than others. It's highly likely that any other potential suitors are automatically erased from your attention or interest. While you may feel having a discussion about being exclusive isn't necessary in your situation, it's still recommended as a way to declare your commitment.

Making your relationship "official" is a fun and bonding milestone. This can happen when you decide to introduce him to your friends and family as your boyfriend, by consistently including him in your life, or even more publicly on social media.

As you begin to join your lives together, it's your right to continue to evaluate how you feel about this man. You're making an investment in your future with this relationship, but you don't need to rush things… enjoy what's evolving. Ask yourself, from a realistic and grounded mindset, if you can truly see yourself with this man for the next 5, 10, 20 years? With what you know of him and your overall experiences together, is he "the one," your forever love?

Finding a New Balance

While you're dating your Mr. Right, you'll likely feel on top of the world– filled with confidence and trust in your new relationship journey. The contentment and happiness you have is like no other, and you surrender to the fact that this is your new normal. Even for the most compatible of soul mates, the excitement will eventually begin to settle and more "real life" matters will become part of your every day.

There may come a time where your wonderful and amazing life feels a bit out of balance. That lopsidedness typically occurs when we've not allowed ourselves time and space to continue doing those other things in life that *we* love. When you're in a wonderful relationship it may seem at first that the world around you doesn't exist, but in time, typical stressors will creep back in, and it's important to allow yourself to nurture your self-care needs and unwind, challenge yourself, and continue to change and grow.

Allow yourself to have alone time, go out with your girlfriends, maybe even travel solo to visit friends, and continue to pursue your goals and dreams.

Your life will continue to transform as your relationship bond grows deeper. Allow time and acceptance for your new identity to take shape– from single lady in search mode to a woman who's found her Mr. Right– and enjoy what that feels like.

Real Life Challenges

This section presents some of the realistic issues you may experience even after finding your forever love. If we're prepared for reality not being perfect, we can manage our passage through the challenges with more grace and stay grounded in our own strength, and the relationship's strength.

When Past Doubts Creep In

It's easy when things are going well to celebrate that, but even in the most seemingly perfect relationships, your past experiences or doubts can creep back in and cause you to wonder if this is too good to be true. These are what I call "mini-freak outs" that can happen, especially if you've never been treated so well by anyone else before. They are normal. Talking through your worries openly with your partner should help the fears subside and help you return to center, so you can let go of the past and focus on the real man before you.

Blending Families

Blending your families, regardless of the ages of the kids, can be challenging. To his kids you might be looked at as an outsider who doesn't fit into what they've been used to. You could be viewed as someone who's stealing or taking too much of their "dad time." An emotionally mature man will be able to tell his kids—even if they don't like it—that this is the woman he has chosen to grow old with and they will need to find a way to accept that and accept you. Or, your kids could be struggling with the merger and are nervous about having step-siblings.

Moving

Merging two households together into one home can result in lots of extra stuff, and it can even feel really overwhelming. Being open to discussing which duplications can be tossed, donated, or sold is an important part of healthy communication. Doing so from a place of openness and what makes the most sense, versus feeling resentful about it, will make the moving process go much smoother.

Job Stress

Working is inevitable if we want to pay our bills and stay in our homes. But each job can have pressures and stresses that even the most self-aware and respectable person can end up bringing home. If your partner is struggling with work stress, your role is not to "fix", but rather to be there for moral support. When you or your partner are stressed, quirks and lack of tolerance of little things can become amplified. Seeing it for what it is—stress coming out in different ways– will help you to better manage yourself so you don't get triggered into a harsh reaction or argument.

Handling One-Off Situations

These are unique and unexpected things that can happen that you may or may not judge your partner for. Job loss and a health crisis are among the top stressors that can impact your new relationship. Both have a direct impact on your finances, which is stressful all on its own. This can also include dealing with a death of a loved one. Regardless of the situation, you want to be able and willing to go through this hard time together, take your turn at being the strong one, and rally to support your partner as you weather the storm. Trusting that everything will work out– that you're a team and in this together– will deepen your relationship bond.

Becoming a United Force

Part of respecting reality involves taking a step back and looking at the complete, overall situation. This can sometimes be referred to as the ten-thousand-foot perspective. Now this is not to be confused with only looking at your relationship, but rather all of the people who are or will be directly impacted by decisions or changes that occur as your new relationship deepens and steps toward long-term permanent commitment begin to take shape.

Megan and Brian were so excited to take the next step in their relationship and move in together. Their homes were on opposite sides of the city from one another. Megan owned a newer starter home, and Brian owned a much larger home that needed some updating and redecorating. The economy was down and only starter homes were selling well on the real estate market, and Brian's house was located in a better school district with a "college prep" high school that was more suitable for Megan's son. They decided to sell Megan's house and then fix up Brian's home.

They had little issue getting everything ready to sell and for the move itself. But the bigger, and very unexpected, issue came up with Megan's son. The night before the move her son had an epic meltdown because he was worried that, with him moving to a new school, his childhood friends wouldn't be able to hang out anymore. Megan and Brian had not even given this potential scenario any thought, because they had been so focused on all the many parts involved with moving.

Seeing this, through the lens of family and realizing this was a *family* issue, helped Megan and Brian quickly figure out a "work around" that would enable her son to stay closely connected with his childhood friends. Once Megan's son heard their solution, he felt relieved and was open to the move the next day. This situation also helped Megan and Brian decide to open up the dialogue by sharing ideas or decisions they were considering that may potentially impact the kids.

This is a very common, yet beneficial learning opportunity, that can occur when you're merging your lives together.

~~~~~~

Respecting reality will help you be better prepared to navigate your new life once you've met your Mr. Right.

In the next chapter, you'll learn about the true value of the FOREVER Framework process.

Chapter 9

Your Transformation

I've given you all of the tactics and strategies in the FOREVER Framework process, but my wish for you— what I really want— is for you to allow yourself to transform. And that starts with learning how to trust your intuition and what you already know, being patient, and dating with confidence, curiosity, and intention.

I want you to really recognize that you have the power and ability to find your Mr. Right— your forever love— and to see yourself for who you really are: a confident woman who's smart, capable, and deserving of an emotionally mature man to build a life with together.

Making the Choice

Finding your source of power comes from choosing to take risks, even when they're scary, and trusting in the process of the FOREVER Framework, implementing the tactics and strategies provided, and learning how to think differently. Thinking differently about yourself, your life, and what you truly want your future to look like is key.

You get the opportunity to truly grow your self-confidence in such a way that you can't help but change. It also includes changing the language you use, and for example, being able to unapologetically say, *"I'm choosing to be selective and patient so I can finally find the man of my dreams... the one I truly deserve."*

Moving Forward

Setting the intention to make changes in your life, committing to the FOREVER Framework process, and then actually doing the work will produce amazing results. You'll have more self-confidence and know how to look for qualities in men to determine if they align with what you truly want, and you'll feel much more content with your life. In addition, you'll be able to continually assess what you truly want in a future relationship, because you'll have a newfound clarity.

There's nothing that teaches you more about *how* to date than choosing to date with intention. And you will start to really learn how to tap into and trust your internal compass of happiness and the certainty that can lead you to finding your Mr. Right sooner.

Your Forever Love

The dream relationship partner you crave is already there waiting for you to find him. You want these things: to feel safe to be yourself, to be treated well, and to feel self-confident. You want support and understanding, and someone to have your back. And you want a place to put your love.

When you start with a new dating strategy, this is where your most amazing transformations will occur. And you'll be poised for magical things to come your way.

Our Transformation

The FOREVER Framework is a new way of seeing dating as a less earth-shattering experience, and instead as a process with intention. It offers a new way to be in romantic relationships and a new way of marriage itself. It also provides a new vision of "ever-aftering" that seeks, with practicality, the true heart in the fairy tale: Forever Love.

Imagine if this became a movement where women stopped falling prey to unhealthy relationships. Where they stopped settling for "not-the-right-fit" relationships. And where they let go of their codependent behaviors. Imagine a world where women date with poise and grounded wisdom, while healing their old wounds and making better choices in the process. Imagine teaching our daughters and sons, by example, about first having a healthy relationship with ourselves so that we can be the best partner in a future relationship. Imagine the trickle-down effect upon our society if women were paired with their Mr. Right, *right away*, and how much happier and healthier our world would be.

My dear, this movement has already begun! Family, friends, and even strangers who've read my first two books—*I Just Want Out* and *Relationship Detox*—have told me how amazed they were by all of the practical and pertinent content I teach. As well as when they shared the framework concepts with others. For example, my hair therapist, Wendi (i.e., my hair stylist), has become my apprentice sharing the concepts I teach clients in my FREEDOM, FORWARD, and FOREVER Frameworks with her clients who have dating or relationship struggles.

Here's a stone in front of you that you can continue to step toward. Just like Wendi, you also have the power to grow this transformational movement and help change lives, too.

Chapter 10

Conclusion

*H*ere we are at the conclusion of your *Finding Forever Love* journey. We've walked through my story of my *30s Gone Wild* dating phase. We discussed what led me to finally wake up and revamp my entire dating strategy. And we went through the detailed steps of the FOREVER Framework process. You learned how to figure out what you want, step into your power, how to take action, what to watch out for and expect along the way, and about what life can look like once you've met your Mr. Right.

My wish for you is that this book has offered inspiration and provided answers to your questions (even to ones you may not have thought of), has filled you with hope, and has given you the strength to find your forever love so you can have an amazing and exciting future!

Where I Am Today

As of the publishing date of this book, over 7 years have passed since I set out on my journey to find *my* Mr. Right.

Because of all of the work I did after stepping out of my *30s Gone Wild* phase, going through a relationship detox, and returning to dating with intention, *I changed*. I changed enough to want more for myself and to understand a lot more about what makes an emotionally healthy relationship. I gave myself permission to embrace being selective and ask the tough questions of my dates. I also stayed focused on myself and on my kids and their needs. I traveled, went to graduate school, and built new healthier friendships.

Even though learning how to change my past habits and fully embrace intentional dating was scary, it taught me so many beneficial lessons. From that experience, I learned:

- About myself—how to trust my intuition and my strength; how my self-worth was not dependent on a

man giving it to me; that I am smart, lovable, and a
sure thing; and about the depth of my perseverance.

- About relationships—what's healthy and what's
unhealthy (including friends and family); how to spot
a sure thing, and how not to allow fear to hold me back
or dictate my dreams and happiness.

A few days after my 40th birthday, I went on a blind date
and met a man who would become my best friend and the
love of my life, Dan. He had a spark about him that I couldn't
forget, and he possessed *all* of the important things I had been
looking for in a life partner. We were married on February 13,
2013, during a sunset ceremony on a beautiful beach in Hawaii.

Since I met Dan, he has been my beacon if ever I feel lost,
my sounding board when I need to vent or want advice, my
cheerleader who always encourages me, my rock supporting me
as I continue to pursue my dreams, and he's a loving step-dad,
great friend, and positive role model for my boys.

I went on to pursue my career goals. I left corporate
America and continue to enjoy adjunct teaching and facilitating
corporate training workshops. Now I'm a Certified Life Coach,
international best-selling author, and speaker who specializes in
relationships and helping to make a difference in other people's
lives. I am so proud to have the ability to share my experience
and to support other women through the empowering journey

and life-changing processes as they pursue their dreams. And I am even more honored to be a leader of such an important transformational movement.

Continue Your Journey with Me

As you've read this book, there may have been others who came to mind that you feel could also benefit from my story and my experience. I invite you to share this book with them.

You can visit www.findingforeverlovebook.com to download the *Finding Forever Love Tool Kit* as you complete the FOREVER Framework process.

If you'd like an experienced companion to walk beside you on your *Finding Forever Love* journey, you can apply for a complimentary relationship clarity session. You will find details on my website at www.findingforeverlovebook.com.

I wish you strength and hope, and send you love and light.

Acknowledgments

First off, I'd like to thank my wonderful husband, Dan, for understanding and accepting my desire to take this huge leap of becoming an author (for the third time) and sharing my relationship experiences, knowledge, and teachings with the world. And for seeing the big picture of how important it is to me to help other women find the same happiness and relationship success that we have. This third book is what ultimately led me to finally finding you—my forever love.

I also want to thank all my past relationships and dates, and my guy-friends who helped teach me what I truly wanted and deserved for my life. The list is extensive, and you know who you are. So, thanks a million for helping make this book possible!

I am grateful to all of my dear friends who provided moral support during my post-divorce single years—they know who they are! Thanks also to my inner circle of friends who've watched me transform from caterpillar to butterfly, multiple times over. I'm grateful for their continued kindness, love, and support. And, for being open-minded and willing to learn from my life experiences. I appreciate them for all the joy and great memories they help create when we're together.

Thanks to my family for encouraging me to find myself and to look at the world through a bigger lens. And for showing me by example, how to step through my fears, trust the process, stand up for myself unapologetically and not settle. To my sons, Alec and Ethan, for thinking it's cool to have a mom who is a relationship coach and author, and for choosing career paths where you, too, can help others improve and change their lives!

I am eternally grateful for the countless clients I've had the pleasure of coaching, who had the courage to face their fears and allow me to walk alongside them during their transformations.

Thank you to Angela Lauria and the entire crew at The Author Incubator for their professionalism, support, and belief in helping authors fulfill their dreams. A special thanks to Grace Kerina, for seeing my vision and helping me shape and massage the content of this book, and for teaching me how to become a better writer. I also want to thank Sky Kier, for all of his enthusiasm, support, and suggestions.

To the Morgan James Publishing team: Special thanks to David Hancock, CEO & Founder for believing in me and my message. To my Author Relations Manager, Margo Toulouse, thanks for making the process seamless and easy. Many more thanks to everyone else, but especially Jim Howard, Bethany Marshall, and Nickcole Watkins.

About the Author

 **Jodi Schuelke** is a Certified Life Coach, international best-selling author, successful entrepreneur, speaker, educator and corporate trainer, and coach mentor. She specializes in helping women struggling with their relationships, to discover breakthroughs so they can experience more freedom and joy in their lives. She is passionate about helping women reclaim their strength, open up new ways of thinking, and listen to and trust their intuition so they can move on from relationships that are no longer serving them and find the relationship of their dreams, the one they truly deserve.

She knows first-hand the struggles of what being in unhealthy relationships looks like and has nearly three decades of first-hand experience: 10 years spent trying to *fix* her emotionally abusive first marriage, going through a divorce, co-parenting with a challenging ex, enduring a tumultuous rebound relationship and break-up, dating again in her late thirties, and journeying to find her dream relationship and getting married again.

Jodi has had the privilege to train and be mentored by some of the most noted coaches in the industry, and holds a Life Coach Certification from the Martha Beck Institute. She also has a master's degree in management and organizational behavior, with an emphasis in training and personal development. In addition to her individual and group coaching, she also utilizes her coaching skills in her role as an adjunct professor and corporate trainer teaching interpersonal communications, career and life transitions, change management, and leadership.

She lives in Wisconsin with her husband, Dan, her two sons and step-children, and a fur-child, Echo the Siberian husky.

Thank You!

Hey, thanks for reading *Finding Forever Love: 7 Steps to Your Mr. Right*. This isn't the end, but rather the beginning of a life-changing and worthwhile journey. I sincerely hope this book has provided you with peace of mind and encouragement as you prepare for finding your Mr. Right.

Download the Free Finding Forever Love Tool Kit

Please visit my website www.findingforeverlovebook.com to download the free *Finding Forever Love Tool Kit* to help as you complete the FOREVER Framework process.

Help Finding Mr. Right

If you'd like an experienced companion to walk beside you on your *Finding Forever Love* journey, you can apply for a complimentary relationship clarity session. You will find details on my website at www.findingforeverlovebook.com.

Books by Jodi Schuelke

Book 1: *I Just Want Out: Seven Careful Steps to Leaving Your Emotionally Abusive Husband*

Book 2: *Relationship Detox: 7 Steps to Prepare for Your Ideal Relationship*

Book 3: *Finding Forever Love: 7 Steps to Your Mr. Right*

CPSIA information can be obtained
at www.ICGtesting.com
Printed in the USA
BVHW032241250919
559464BV00001B/6/P

9 781642 793468